# Writing Essays:
## what you need to know

L E Jenkinson

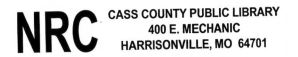

Visit **blackboardfiction.com** for more writing tips, advice and fun!

# Writing Essays

Welcome to what will hopefully be an invaluable writing guide for you! These resources have been developed with students to find the most effective presentation of the facts and skills needed for essay-writing, from KS3 to GCSE to A-Level and perhaps beyond.

This guide will prepare you from the ground up, building on each layer of knowledge and skills, fully equipping you for confident essay-writing and filling in any gaps in your knowledge along the way.

## Contents

## INDEX of different essay styles and structures

**About the author:**

L. E. Jenkinson is a teacher, tutor, writer, artist, and firm believer that a little help goes a long way.

WWW.LAURAJENKINSON.COM

# 1: Essay Punctuation and Grammar and where to use it

## Punctuation

There are twelve major pieces of punctuation that you need to be able to use competently in order to get the best marks for your work and make it as legible as possible. They are all explored on the next pages with their rules and examples of use.

What are they and how are they used?

# Essay punctuation:

**FULL STOP.** A full stop:
— **ends a sentence**.
✎ Full stops **go inside quotation marks if they are part of the original quotation**.

**COMMA.** A comma:
— **ends clauses (sections of a sentence)**, separating them from each other (see the section on Sentence Structure).
— **separates items in a list** (*The sisters were Anne, Lucinda and Debbie.*)
✎ Commas go inside quotation marks if they are part of the original quotation.
✎ Commas go inside speech marks if the sentence is continued (*"You're insulting my sister," said Dave.*)

**COLON.** A colon **introduces**:
— **a list** (*There were three sisters: Anne, Lucinda and Debbie.*)
— **a clause that affects (e.g.: adds to) the previous clause** (*He had several sisters: Anne was one of them.*) (see p.16 for clauses)
✎ The word following a colon does not need a capital letter unless it is a proper noun (a name or place).

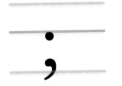

## SEMICOLON. These **introduce**:

— **items in a list which have punctuation in them** (*There were three sisters: Anne, who was the stubborn one; Lucinda, who was the quiet one; and Debbie, who was odd.*)

— **a clause that adds information to the previous clause, used instead of a connective** (*There were three sisters; we only knew one of them.*)

✎ The word following does not need a capital letter unless it is a proper noun.

## APOSTROPHE. An apostrophe:

— **shows a contraction**, where letters are missing/have been removed (*They are = they're.*)

— **indicates possession** (*The boy's sisters.*)

— **shows something that already ends in an 's' as a plural** (*The sisters of the boys = the boys' sisters.*)

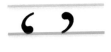

## QUOTATION MARKS I. Single marks:

— called *inverted commas*, **show speech or quoted speech/text.**

✎ As a rule of style, inverted commas are often used to show popular phrases, e.g.: thinking 'outside the box'.

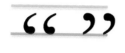

**QUOTATION MARKS II.** Double marks show:
— **speech or quoted speech/text**.

 As a rule of style, double quotation marks are normally used to show actual speech and quotations, rather than popular phrases, and can be used to show speech within speech (*'You called my sister Debbie "the odd one",'* *said Dave.*)

**HYPHEN/DASH.**
— A **hyphen** is used to join words or to link single syllables of words (*'to-morrow' was the original form of 'tomorrow'*).
— A **dash** is longer than a hyphen and shows a sudden break in a line (*Debbie was – he jumped when he realised what he was seeing*), or an interjection (*"Debbie, what are you – oh!"*)

**ELLIPSIS.** Ellipses are used to:
— **show missed-out words in a quotation** where it is too long to write the whole thing out but you want to indicate that it is all important.
— **show unfinished speech or thought or a slow tailing-off** (*"Debbie is…. I don't want to talk about it…"*)

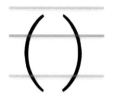

**BRACKETS (PARENTHESES).** Brackets:

— are **used to show extra information.**

✎ In essays, we use commas around subordinate clauses to do this instead of using brackets, but information such as the author of a book or a page number can be added in brackets after quotations in an essay.

**QUESTION MARK.** A question mark:

— **indicates that a question is being asked**.

✎ Another indicator to show this is word order (*The sisters are in the house. Are the sisters in the house?*)

**EXCLAMATION MARK.**

The exclamation (Latin: 'he shouts out') **indicates**:

— **excitement, caused by fear or happiness,** in a speaker.

— **high volume**.

— **an unusual outcome**.

✎ Exclamation marks are not usually used in formal essays (except when in quotation) as *analysis is scientific, not emotional.*

# Other punctuation notes:

 This is an <u>ampersand</u>.
It is used to replace the word 'and'.
It is used in shop signs and company titles, such as 'Dunder & Dunder Solicitors'.
**On no account is it to be used as 'and' in formal essay writing.**

TENSES

You should write *about* texts, poems and plays in the **present tense,** <u>not</u> the past tense.
This is because if text events and characters were to be referred to in the past then they would sound like historical events.
Using the present tense reflects the nature of a text; *it happens as you read it.*
e.g.: *'The character tells the other character that they are feeling "low", and then leaves.'*

NUMBERS AND NUMERALS

As a rule of style, **numbers under 100 should be written as words**.
When describing plays, Roman numerals are used to describe Acts and Scenes (e.g.: Act II Scene III)

# PARAGRAPHS, CAPITALS AND FULL STOPS

**PARAGRAPHS** are groups of sentences that make up prose texts (not *poetry*: we use *stanzas* for that).

You **start a new paragraph each time you change the**:

## Ti P To P

**Ti**me – in creative writing, the setting
**P**lace – in creative writing, the setting
**To**pic – in essays, each point you make
**P**erson – in creative writing, the speaker

**CAPITAL LETTERS** are used:
- for the **first word in a sentence**
- for **proper nouns** (*see parts of speech*)

**FULL STOPS** are used:
- at the **end of sentences**
(make sure you don't actually need a comma – *look at the section on sentence structure*)

**That's really all there is to it on these. Make using them a priority!**

's' for skull

'B' for Bert

# The Parts of Speech

Or, the most common types of words and their families. You need to know what these are and how to use them in essays – as well as being able to spot them to discuss the way authors use them.

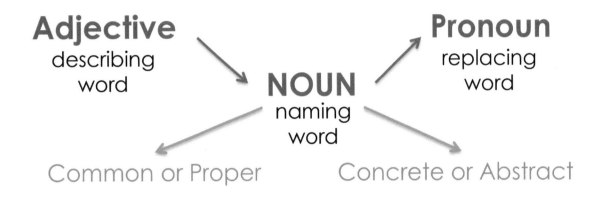

**Adjective**
describing word

**NOUN**
naming word

**Pronoun**
replacing word

Common or Proper

Concrete or Abstract

**PREPOSITION**
placing word

**CONJUNCTION**
joining word

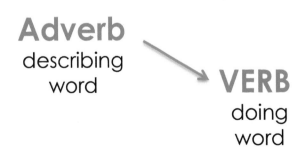

**Adverb**
describing word

**VERB**
doing word

# Adjective

Describing word for nouns; **big, small, blue, leathery, chocolatey, friendly, rubbery, loud,** etc. Using these can help build up a picture for your reader.

Essay naming words might be **author, text, poem, novel, device, effect, technique, conclusion, character, link, evidence, example, type, object, idea, summary, protagonist.**

# NOUN

# Pronoun

Replacing word for nouns; **her, she** for female nouns, **him, his** for male nouns, **it, their** for neuter nouns.
Using these will stop your work from being repetitive, and help you establish the Subject and Object in sentences.

## Common or Proper

Common nouns are **labels,** such as **teacher, dog, city.**
Proper nouns are **proper names,** such as **Miss Lemon, Mina** and **London.**
(As you can see, proper nouns start with a *capital letter.*)

## Concrete or Abstract

Concrete nouns are **tangible** (touchable, sensed with the five senses) things, like **table, roses,** and, well, **concrete.**
Abstract nouns are **intangible** things (that cannot be sensed with your five senses) like ideas and concepts, like **beauty, bravery, trust.**

## PREPOSITION

A placing word that tells your reader the **position of a noun** and its relationship to the rest of the sentence, such as **in, on, through, before.** The noun becomes the object of the preposition, so normally follows it. In an essay, you will use it to establish where evidence comes from or locate a text section for discussion.

## CONJUNCTION

A linking word (often called a connective) that links nouns, verbs or clauses together, most often **and, or, nor, but, yet, for, also, so, because.** There are different types you'll find in essays:

coordinating (linking items of the same value: 'him **and** her');

correlative (pairs of conjunctions that coordinate: '**Either** him **or** her…';

subordinating (introducing clauses dependent on the previous clause: 'He is, **although** she isn't') which will be important in explaining the effects of things like language devices: 'The author uses strong verbs **in order that** the action is vivid'.

## Adverb

A describing word for verbs that tells how the verb is being done, like **quickly, slowly, intuitively, apprehensively, carefully, forcefully, amusingly.** They often end in **–ly.**
In an essay, adverbs can be useful for evaluating the effect of something: 'The author uses this device **effectively**…'

## VERB
### doing word

Essay doing words might be **writes, explores, develops, continues, chooses, uses, elaborates, explains, orchestrates, creates, maintains, characterises, emphasises, analyses.**

# 2: Sentence Structure

Haven't a clue what to 'vary sentences' with? Using different types of sentence in your essays will both improve your grade by showing skill and make your essay more interesting to read for the examiner.

## Things you need to know first:

Sentences have **three basic parts**

| The **subject** | The **VERB** | The **object** |
| --- | --- | --- |
| This is what the sentence is **about** | This is what the subject is **doing** | This is what the subject is doing the verb **to.** |

# The cat sat on the mat.

The **subject**

The **subject** of the sentence is **what the sentence is about** – a **noun** (Here it's a <u>cat.</u>)

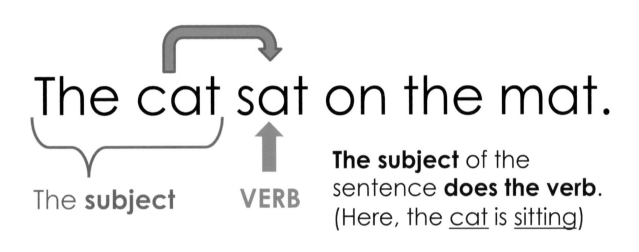

The **subject**　VERB

**The subject** of the sentence **does the verb**. (Here, the <u>cat</u> is <u>sitting</u>)

The **subject**　VERB　The **object**

**The object** of the sentence **has the verb done to it** – **another noun** (The <u>mat</u> has the <u>cat</u> <u>sitting</u> on it.)

# Other stuff you should know:

clause - a part of a sentence

main sentence clause - the main part of the sentence with the verb in it.

# Now you're ready to start:

There are <u>three</u> main types of sentence you need to use

1. Simple sentences

   (The cat sat on the mat.)

2. Compound sentences

   (The cat sat on the mat **and** eyed the goldfish.)

3. Complex sentences

   (The cat, **which was getting hungry**, eyed the goldfish.)

# 1. Simple sentences

The cat sat on the mat.

**One thing did one thing to one thing.**

(That's it.)

The skull sat on the books. Obviously.

# 2. Compound sentences

In Science, a compound is made of **two elements** joined together by a **chemical reaction**.

A compound. Can you see the join?

Compound sentences are made of **simple sentences** joined together (connected) with a **conjunction (connective) like 'and', 'or', 'but'**.

**simple sentence**

**simple sentence**

The cat sat on the mat.    The cat eyed the goldfish.

The cat sat on the mat **and** eyed the goldfish.

**compound sentence**    CONNECTIVE

# 3. Complex sentences

Complex sentences get...
complicated.

There is a **main clause**, where the **verb, the subject and the object** are.

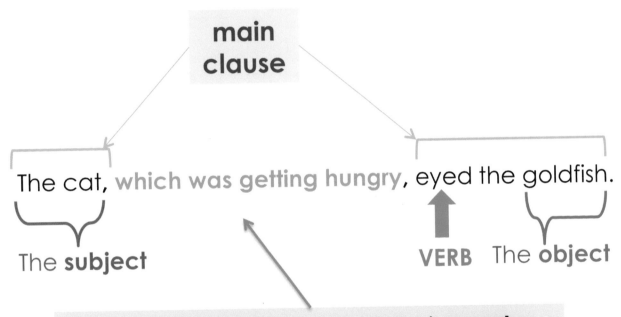

**main clause**

The cat, **which was getting hungry**, eyed the goldfish.

The **subject**

VERB    The **object**

This is a 'subordinate clause'. It gives **extra** information: 'subordinate' means 'lower than the main...lower-ranking', so we know this is not part of the main clause, but instead **supports it. Commas** are put round it, **like brackets**, to show that it is **extra**.

There are **other clauses** (subordinate clauses) that give **extra information**.

# Subordinate clauses depend on the main sentence to make sense – **they do not make sense on their own.**

See?

**which was getting hungry**

This means nothing. There is no <u>subject</u> or <u>object</u> for it to relate to.

The cat, **which was getting hungry,** eyed the goldfish.

**The main clause gives <u>a reason for</u> the subordinate clause.**

**The subordinate clause gives <u>extra meaning to</u> the main clause.**

NOTE: this is why you may NOT begin a sentence (main clause) with a **connective** or **relative pronoun (unless you are asking a question)**, as these are used to introduce subordinate clauses!

Connectives:
and or but because
although (more later)

Relative pronouns:
who whom which whose
whoever whosoever
whomever what whatever
that

Before you read the next page, read this:

# EXTRA: How to use 'because'

| EFFECT | | CAUSE |
|--------|---|-------|
| Something happened... | ...**because**... | ...something caused it to happen. |
| It was my birthday... | ...**because**... | ...another year had passed. |
| You are going to write a good essay... | ...**because**... | ...you have studied this guide well. |
| We feel pathos for the character... | ...**because**... | ...the author has created them to be sympathetic. |

'Because' *links* the **cause** and the **effect**.

Therefore, you **may not have one without the other** in a sentence.

The **most common error** made in essay sentence structure is using connectives at the beginning of sentences, like 'which', 'but', 'because', 'and':

The cat is described as 'hungry'. Which suggests it wants to eat the fish.

NO!

❌

The cat is described as 'hungry', which suggests it wants to eat the fish.

**main clause**

**The subordinate clause gives extra meaning to the main clause. A comma shows it Is linked.**

✓

Examples of using 'because' in different positions:

Because the fish is described as 'hungry', the cat appears to want to eat the fish.

'Because' starts the sentence as it starts the subordinate clause. It gives **a reason for the main clause.**

The cat, because it is described as hungry, appears to want to eat the fish.

'Because' starts the subordinate clause and **introduces it after the first part of the main clause**. 'The fish' is switched for the pronoun 'it', because 'the fish' has been introduced in the main clause; 'it' relates to it.

The cat appears to want to eat the fish because it is described as 'hungry'.

'Because' is a connective, and here **it connects two simple sentences to make a compound sentence** *instead* of starting a subordinate clause. This happens as 'because' suggests a **result/effect**.

**READ THESE OUT LOUD TO *HEAR* EACH CLAUSE**

# How examiners see sentence structure:

'Varying your sentences' in *analytical essays* means that if you **use a mix of these three types**, you will **get a better mark.**

'Varying your sentences' in *creative writing* means that if you **use a mix of these types of sentences *to create effects***, you will **get a better mark:**

SIMPLE SENTENCES: are short and build suspense when they are layered one after the other.

*He stopped.*

COMPOUND SENTENCES: when kept to two sentences/clauses, have a similar effect to simple sentences but give more information.

*He stopped and looked round.*

COMPLEX SENTENCES: can be used to set the scene with lots of description and additional 'back-story' information…and lull readers into a false sense of security that you can then shock them out of with a short, simple sentence!

*He stopped and looked round at the house, which had once been a place of happiness but now looked sad and empty. Suddenly there was a noise behind him…*

# 3: Analysing the Question and Planning an Essay

The skills in this section teach you how to really work out what the essay question is asking you to do, and what your teacher or examiner is expecting you to write, making sure that all of your hard work pays off when you actually answer the question!

## First: work out what your essay is about by analysing the question!

First of all, let's look at the kind of questions you're likely to come up against:

Example basic essay question formula:

How does the author/poet/playwright present/portray/develop/explore/use

the particular character/ particular theme/ particular technique in the novel/poem/play ?

With any essay question or task, you should be able to pick out **key words** that tell you **HOW** to answer the question and what to **FOCUS** on.

'How' tells you **HOW** to answer the question (funnily enough): it means 'explain the techniques the writer uses'. *(There are more examples on the next page of '**HOW**' INSTRUCTIONS)*

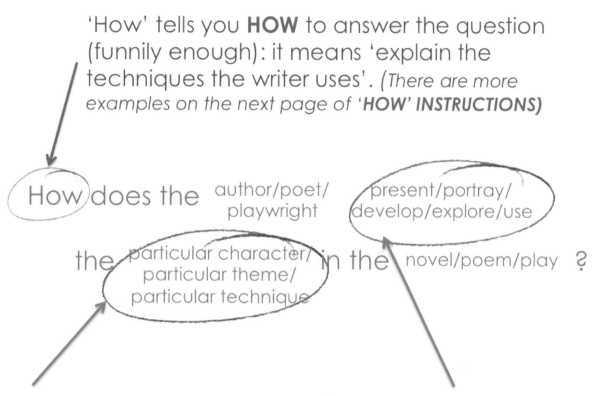

How does the author/poet/playwright present/portray/develop/explore/use

the particular character/ particular theme/ particular technique in the novel/poem/play ?

The feature of the text specified for you to explain is the **FOCUS,** and you only need to choose information from the text that is related to this feature.

This is the **MAIN FOCUS** of your essay and your **plan** will center on it – **every paragraph** should be about an aspect of it.

The verbs used to describe what the author has done are part of the **FOCUS**. They specify the techniques and effects you should be explaining.

This is the **FOCUS LINK.** You will need to **explain** how the author achieves this verb, and use it **to LINK back to the question** at the end of your paragraphs.

# 'HOW' key words you are likely to get in analytical essay questions:

discuss = find a range of points that support the FOCUS part of the question, possibly including a for/against argument.

explain/ describe how = provide points that support the point being made by the FOCUS part of the question.

how...? = the same as 'explain' but phrased as a question.

how effectively ...? = you need to *evaluate* the way the author has done something.

compare/ contrast = look at similar or different points in whatever FOCUS areas the question states, eg: two poems with the theme of 'memory', two characters in a novel.

why...? = this is also the same as 'explain', with generally a smaller FOCUS area.

How far do **you** agree that...?

In light of this statement, what do **you** think?...

= These types of questions will give you a point of view/ statement against which to consider the text. It's not really asking for your *personal* opinion, but your *analytical* opinion; explain and back up your answer, giving an argument **for and against** the statement.

# Next: make a plan based on the FOCUS points

There are different planning styles to use, but the principle is the same – **you are making a checklist of ideas to put in your essay.**

There is a saying:

### "If you FAIL TO PLAN, you PLAN TO FAIL."

This is, in fact, pretty much true; if you don't write down your ideas before you start, **you are extremely likely to miss things out or forget to write about them**. However, if you plan before writing your essay, you are actually **engaging your brain with the question, and you are likely to think of more points to write about**. You are also going to be able **to put your points in a more logical order** which will **strengthen your argument**, and **your conclusion is going to be easier to write.**

 If you're one of those people who thinks 'But, the examiner isn't going to mark my plan,' or, 'Yes, but I plan as I go along,' **you still need to plan**: some exam boards now allow their examiners to look at the plan and give credit for anything in it that the student ran out of time to say in the essay. **So there.**

### PLANNED ESSAYS ARE **ALWAYS** BETTER.

# TYPES OF PLAN

(Spider diagrams arrange ideas like **spider legs**)

## Spider diagram/ Mindmap:

author presents something in each chapter

author uses technique to show something

ESSAY QUESTION: how does author do something?

author uses character to do something

author uses something to represent something else

each thing represented links to a theme

Different characters do this in different ways

(Mindmaps **link and grow ideas further**, like branches on a tree)

## Bullet points:

Q: how does author do something?

 - author uses technique to show something

 - author presents something in each chapter

 - author uses different characters to show something

(Bullet points are **lists** of ideas)

It's not important what order you put your ideas in at first – when you're finished you should **go back and number your points in a logical order** for your essay.

# Popular (*ahem*) questions:

### How does the writer....? A.K.A. EXPLAIN EFFECTS

This question asks for a specific topic to be explored and the methods of the author in that area explained. The basic essay structure will work here.

### In this extract....? A.K.A. CLOSE REFERENCE

A little like 'How does the writer…?', this focuses on a specific passage or extract from a text instead of a theme or topic. Either work chronologically through it, explaining effects, or write about how specific effects are achieved/used throughout the extract. *Often called a 'passage' or 'gobbet' question.*

### How far do you agree....? A.K.A. FOR AND AGAINST

This is a challenge: create a balanced and compelling argument that draws to a natural conclusion, Normally some kind of stimulation will be given, such as an inflammatory suggestion or a reference to the text's context. You must try and argue both sides, but one will generally be more obviously 'true' than the other.

### To what extent....? A.K.A. (DIS)PROVING THE STATEMENT

This similarly asks you to argue for or against a point of view, and again you must make sure you treat both sides of the argument. For both of these questions, start with the side that convinces you least, then undermine it with the stronger.

# 4: Paragraph Structure

How to structure your analytical paragraphs. There is, in fact, a trick to it, and once you know how to do it simply, you can swap it round to make your paragraphs sound even more sophisticated – and interesting to the examiner!

## First: work out what your essay is about!

Your essay plan should look something like this:

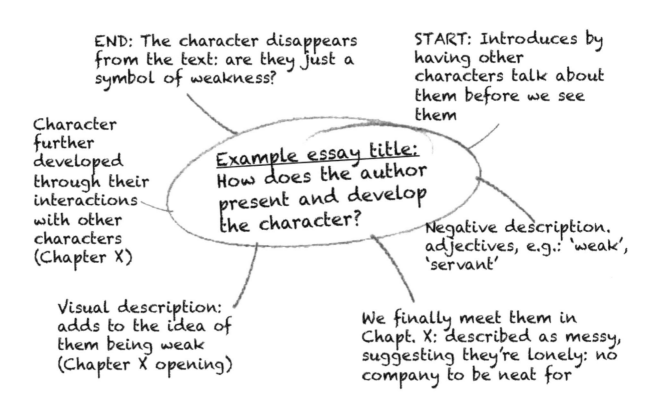

END: The character disappears from the text: are they just a symbol of weakness?

START: Introduces by having other characters talk about them before we see them

Character further developed through their interactions with other characters (Chapter X)

Example essay title: How does the author present and develop the character?

Negative description. adjectives, e.g.: 'weak', 'servant'

Visual description: adds to the idea of them being weak (Chapter X opening)

We finally meet them in Chapt. X: described as messy, suggesting they're lonely: no company to be neat for

Each of these points will become a **paragraph**, or more than one paragraph, of your essay.

# Your paragraphs will have three parts:

# P.E.E.

## Point (P.)

Make your overall paragraph point – it should be something that supports your overall answer.

## Evidence (Ev.)

Give your proof for your point - this should be a quotation from the text your essay is about. It should support what you're trying to say in your Point.

## Explanation (Ex.)

Link your evidence to your point
or
explain the connotations
or
summarise the relevance of your evidence

You can also add another section:
**Link** – link back to the overall Essay question to really make sure what you've written is relevant!

# P.

Make your overall paragraph point – it should be something that supports your overall answer.

## Simple example:

> The character is presented at first through other characters.

# Ev.

Give your proof for your point - this should be a quotation from the text your essay is about. It should support what you're trying to say in your Point.

> Bert calls him "the outcast", and "that guy" when describing him to the newcomers in Chapter X.

# Ex.

Link your evidence to your point
or
explain the connotations
or
summarise the relevance of your evidence

> The reader is immediately meant to think of the character as different, and not known well by the others who think of him as just "that guy".

# P.

Make your overall paragraph point – it should be something that supports your overall answer.

## More detailed example:

> The character is **presented at first through other characters**.

only make **one point** at a time – you can always write more paragraphs!

# Ev.

Give your proof for your point - this should be a quotation from the text your essay is about. It should support what you're trying to say in your Point.

> Bert calls him **"the outcast"**, and **"that guy"** when describing him to the newcomers in Chapter X.

You can use more than one piece of evidence to support the same point.

**Integrate** your short quotations so that they fit into the sentence
*(there's more on quotations later on in this book)*

# Ex.

Link your evidence to your point
or
explain the connotations
or
summarise the relevance of your evidence

> The reader is immediately meant to think of the character **as different, and not known well by the others who think of him as just "that guy".**

The **connotations are explained** for each quotation, and linked back to the essay title.

As you get used to including the three parts of the P.E.E. structure in each paragraph, you'll find that you are able to write more fluently without thinking about the three parts individually.

However, to make absolutely certain that you're being as analytical as possible and answering the question, **you can use the P.E.E structure as a quick content checklist.**

**Look at this example of a more sophisticated version of the 'simple example';** can you identify the Point, Evidence (in several explained examples), and the Explanation?

The character is presented at first through other characters. The reader is immediately meant to think of the character as different, and not known well by the others who think of him as just "him". For example, Bert calls him "the outcast", and "that guy" when describing him to the newcomers in Chapter X, immediately marking him out as separate. Similarly, Arthur doesn't have him written on the "list of original recruits", perhaps suggesting that he joined up at another time from the others and so wasn't part of the original group.

Answer:

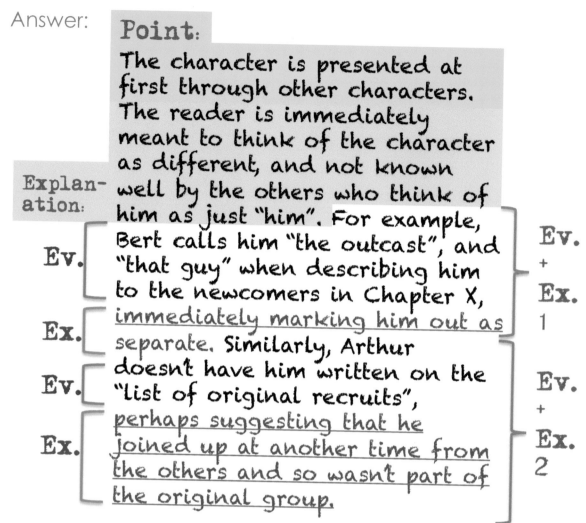

**Point:**
The character is presented at first through other characters. The reader is immediately meant to think of the character as different, and not known well by the others who think of him as just "him". For example, Bert calls him "the outcast", and "that guy" when describing him to the newcomers in Chapter X, <u>immediately marking him out as separate.</u> Similarly, Arthur doesn't have him written on the "list of original recruits", <u>perhaps suggesting that he joined up at another time from the others and so wasn't part of the original group.</u>

**Explanation:**

Ev.

Ex.

Ev.

Ex.

Ev. + Ex. 1

Ev. + Ex. 2

The Point has stayed in the same place, introducing the paragraph. This is probably the most **effective** place for it to be.

The Evidence is now made up of two sets of explained quotations, meaning that the point is being made more **thoroughly and confidently**.

The Explanation is now near the start of the paragraph. It is still giving a **mini-conclusion** to the paragraph and **explaining the effect of the Evidence**.

**Playing with the structure like this will make your essay seem less formulaic** (repetitive and 'samey') **and more sophisticated.**

# FACT: If you don't Explain, you are NOT ANALYSING

...and so won't get above a D or a C. Explaining is the KEY to getting a B or above.

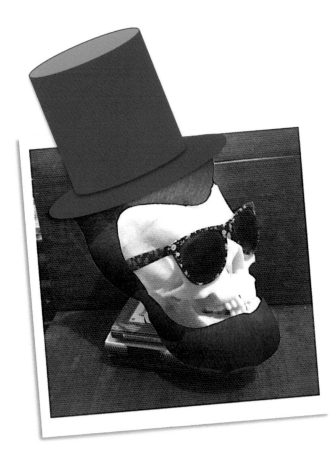

old **ABE** says...

**A**lways **B**e **E**xplaining!

Bert idolises
Abe Lincoln.
No, really.

# 5: Using Quotations as Evidence

When analysing texts, you won't get far if you don't look at the language being used and the effect it is having on the reader, and then include it in your paragraphs. Remember this: every word has been chosen by the author for a reason. Find that reason. Tell us about it. Get a good grade.

## Analysis practice:

What can we explain about these pieces of evidence?

"I can't believe you broke the window and you didn't say anything! You're not even saying anything now! How can you stand there and look at me with that look on your face?"

"Nothing more strongly arouses our disgust than cannibalism, yet we make the same impression on Buddhists and vegetarians, for we feed on babies, though not our own".

"Don't you think it's time for a change? You've worked so hard, all of you, and for what? You've got nothing to show for it, and someone else has taken all the credit. Well, I think you should strike. Strike! And ask for better pay, better working conditions, and credit for the work you do!"

# Explaining Evidence:

Below are some very developed explanations of the evidence from the previous page, and a point they could be used to support.

**Point:** The speaker is angry and surprised at the actions of another person.

**Explanation of the evidence:** The speaker uses simple sentences and exclamation marks to show their emotion of surprise at what has happened. They repeatedly explain or suggest how they feel: "I can't believe you broke the window and didn't say anything! You're not even saying anything now!" They also use a rhetorical question to highlight how the other person's behaviour is wrong; "How can you stand there...?"

**Point:** Eating meat is hypocritical as it is akin to (like) cannibalism.

**Explanation of the evidence:** Robert Louis Stevenson likens eating meat to "eating babies, though not our own", and says this would be as shocking to humans who are vegetarians or Buddhists, both parties who are against eating meat, as cannibalism is to the majority of humans.

**Point:** The speaker is trying to motivate someone or a group to take action.

**Explanation of the evidence:** The speaker uses rhetorical questions to suggest a route of action to the listener, "Don't you think it's time for a change?" and adds a statement to strengthen the negative feeling created; "You've got nothing to show for it, and someone else has taken all the credit." They then give their opinion, repeating it with an order to "Strike!" before telling the listener the exact course of action to take.

# How to use quotations effectively:

In short: write a **lot** about a **little**.

In the examples on the previous page, each piece of evidence had the most important features and effects in it explained and explored.

Here's a breakdown of the first piece of evidence, showing how much you can say about tiny details:

Personal pronouns 'I', 'me' and 'you' are repeated, telling us this is a direct conversation between two people, and could be quite intimate. 'You' is the most repeated, suggesting that the speaker is not letting the other get a word in, so is perhaps angry.

"I can't believe you broke the window and you didn't say anything! You're not even saying anything now! How can you stand there and look at me with that look on your face?"

This question mark is actually showing a rhetorical question instead of a real one, which adds to the effect of the person being angry; they are clearly trying to make a point.

There are several uses of exclamation marks, telling us that the speaker is very excited.

Even without writing about sentence length or the words used (as in the example), **a lot of information has already been found to be written about!**

# Two ways of getting quotations into your writing:

## Introduction or Integration

**1: Introduce your quotations with a semicolon.** This will show that your quotation is a continuation of the earlier part of the sentence, which will contain your point. Be careful not to be repetitive though!

> In the extract, the speaker is clearly angry; "How can you stand there and look at me...?" they ask the other character accusatorially. They also repeat a direct pronoun; "You...you..." This emphasises the anger being directed at the other character.

**2: Integrate your quotations into your sentences by building a sentence around it that makes sense.** This will help you discuss shorter quotations, and will look sophisticated as you will be supporting your ideas directly and without repetition.

> In the extract, the speaker angrily asks "How can you stand there and look at me...?", sounding quite accusatory. The repetition of "you" also adds to the accusing and angry tone.

Use a combination of these techniques in your essay to show off a truly sophisticated style.

# 6: Essay Structure

Once you know how to structure an analytical paragraph, you need to know how to put your paragraphs together so they build up an argument that answers the title question.

## Similarities:

Like your paragraphs, your essay has three parts:

## P.E.E.

### Point
Make your overall point

### Evidence
Give your proof for your point

### Explanation
Link your evidence to your point
or
explain the connotations
or
summarise the relevance of
your evidence

## I.B.C

### Introduction
Briefly answer the question
(Make your overall point)

### Body
Your PEE paragraphs go here

(Give your proof for your point)

### Conclusion
Summarise all of your points to
show how you have answered
the question
or
summarise the relevance of
your evidence

Basically , they're the **same** structure.

# Basic content:

**I.**

Briefly answer the question
(Make your overall point)

| Analyse the question and use words from it to create your introductory sentence. |
| --- |

**B.**

Your P.E.E. paragraphs go here

(Give proof for your

point)

Make each point in its own paragraph.

You'll need to make a plan of all the points you're going to make and the order you're going to put them in, depending on the type of essay you are writing.

Your body paragraphs are the longest part of the essay – the filling.

**NOTE:** NEVER EVER use the phrase 'The author (does something) in many different ways' as a shortcut to introduce an essay or paragraph – it means nothing and examiners HATE it. It is much better to use FOCUS words or SUSTIT *(see Index: Analytical essays)* instead.

**C.**

Summarise all of your points to show how you have answered the question
or
summarise the relevance of your evidence

Finalise your overall point. Summarise it, but don't repeat it.

This is the most difficult bit, so have patience! See the tips on the next page…

# An example of basic content:

Essay Q: Explain how the author **does something (in this example: 'How does the author present a certain character?')**

**I.** Intro: The author presents the character as…(use **words from the question to show your focus**, and **give an overall viewpoint of the character** from what you've found in your plan.)

**B.** For this type of **simple essay structure**, you will need to make a list of points about the way the character has been presented, e.g.: appearance, personality, actions and speech, and the connotations of the author's word choices (see 'Using Quotations').

For this type of essay style, **put these paragraphs in the order the reader gets to them in the book** (chronological order).

**C.** Summarise what the character is like – **what have you said about them in the Body?**

To push your conclusion further, get you a better mark and give you something to write about, use this space to say WHY the author did this,

Eg: The author has presented the character in this way so that the reader sympathises with them all the way through the text, creating tension each time they are affected badly by the novel's events.

# 7: Essay Writing Words and Phrases

Stuck for inspiration? Not sure how to make your essays sound more interesting? Worried about repeating yourself? Use these.

The following examples are words and phrases that can be inserted at the **beginning of sentences**, or can be used **to link sentences**, and direct and focus your writing.

**Beginning sentences:** these types of words and phrases are shown with a **capital letter** at the beginning (to start the sentence), and are mostly **subordinate clauses**, shown by the **comma** that comes directly after them to link them to the main sentence you will write.

**Linking sentences:** these words and phrase are shown with an **ellipsis (…)** to show you where to continue the sentence. Those with an **ellipsis either side** can go in-between two sentences to link them as **a compound sentence**, and those with a **comma i**n front and an **ellipsis after** can be used to create a **complex sentence**.

# JOINING WORDS AND PHRASES

to link

      : **similar** ideas

      : **simple sentences** to make **compound sentences**

| | |
|---|---|
| …and… | In addition,… |
| , also… | Furthermore,… |
| …or… | Moreover,… |
| , again… | Besides,… |
| , as well as… | Likewise,… |

# COMPARING YOUR IDEAS:

to link

      : **similar** ideas that do the **same** thing

      : **different** ideas that do the **same** thing

| | |
|---|---|
| In comparison,,… | Also,… |
| On the other hand, … | Similarly,… |
| By contrast,… | In the same way, … |

# CONTRASTING YOUR IDEAS

to link

: **different** ideas that do **different** things

, although…

, but….

, yet, conversely…

, even though…

, despite…

, however…

In contrast,…

In spite of,…

On the contrary,

…

On one hand,…

On the other

hand…

Nevertheless,…

Nonetheless,…

Notwithstanding,…

Regardless of…. , …

Still,…

Yet,…

Notwithstanding the fact that it wasn't daylight, Bert kept his sunglasses on.

# PROVIDING EXAMPLES

to link:

## : your POINT to your EVIDENCE

, for example, "…"

This is shown by…

, for instance, "…"

The author writes that…

To illustrate this, "…"

OR

The following example shows…

The author's words tell us this ; "…"

The author's choice of words shows…

(use a semicolon [ ; ] to introduce your quotation)

# EXPLAINING EXAMPLES

to link:

### :your **EVIDENCE** to your **EXPLANATION**

This shows that...
(obvious implications)

...showing that...

This implies that...
(subtle implications)

...implying that...

This suggests that...
(subtle implications)

...suggesting that...

the author is...
...showing...
(obviously)
...implying...
(subtly)
...suggesting...
(subtly)

...meaning that...

...creating the effect of/that...

(you can replace 'This' with 'which' to connect sentences instead of starting a new one)

...making us think/feel...

# MAKING A CONCESSION
## (a counter-argument)

to link:

**: your IDEAS to a DIFFERENT idea which *challenges* yours - which you should then undermine (prove wrong) to make your argument seem stronger!**

Although it could be said that...

It may appear that...

Of course, on the other hand...

Another interpretation could be...

Some people might think/say...

From another point of view...

# MAKING A CONCLUSION
## (without directly saying so)
to link:
### : your IDEAS to your QUESTION
### : your BODY to your CONCLUSION

As a

consequence,…

As a result,…

Because of….., ….

Therefore, …

On the whole, …

Thus,…

Consequently,…

After all,…

In summary,…

(or just start your
conclusion by linking
back to the original
question.)

# INDEX: essay structures

## ANALYTICAL ESSAY STRUCTURE

This is the basic analytical structure for use with English and English Literature texts, although it can also be modified for other types of text.

Use the parts of the text list opposite to create a **plan.**

You can break any text into these parts:

# S U S T I T

*I've 'SUSTIT' (sussed it) out!*

**S**ummary
**U**nusual Language (techniques)
**S**tructure (and layout)
**T**hemes (those big ideas)
**I**magery (the images/sounds created)
**T**one (the emotion created by the imagery)

Start with the **BIGGEST** things first and work down:

Introduction – **SUMMARISE** text **Focus,** referring to key words which will probably be a **THEME**

First Section – discuss any **STRUCTURE** techniques that link to the **Focus**

Second Section – discuss any **UNUSUAL LANGUAGE** techniques that link to the **Focus**

Third Section – discuss what **IMAGERY** is created by the **UNUSUAL LANGUAGE**, and link it to the **Focus**

Fourth Section –discuss the **TONE** created by the **IMAGERY**, and link it to the **Focus**

use for:
**EXPLAIN EFFECTS** and **CLOSE REFERENCE** essays

CONCLUSION –give a brief summary of the key points you made to finally answer the Focus Instruction, then say **Why** the author has done this.

# COMPARATIVE ESSAY STRUCTURES

The examples here show poems being compared, but instead could be used for any text or work.

**You will discuss similar and different points between several texts.**

## BLOCK STRUCTURE

**Introduction** – briefly summarise poems, referring to key words (FOCUS)

**First Section** – POEM ONE – go through the features of SUSTIT that help you discuss the key words (several paragraphs)

**Second Section** – POEM TWO – go through the features of SUSTIT that help you discuss the key words (several paragraphs)

**CONCLUSION** –give a brief summary of the key points of comparison, then give a personal preference or try and write about why there were differences in the way the poets used the FOCUS.

## FEATURE BY FEATURE STRUCTURE

**Introduction** – briefly summarise poems, referring to key words (FOCUS)

**First Section** – discuss both poems' STRUCTURE in relation to the FOCUS

**Second Section** – discuss both poems' UNUSUAL LANGUAGE in relation to the FOCUS

**Third Section** – discuss both poems IMAGERY created by the UNUSUAL LANGUAGE, in relation to the FOCUS

**Fourth Section** – discuss both poems' TONE created by the IMAGERY, in relation to the FOCUS

**CONCLUSION** –give a brief summary of the key points of comparison, then give a personal preference or try and write about why there were differences in the way the poets used the FOCUS.

## SUMMARY ESSAY STRUCTURE

A summary essay **shows that you have understood a larger essay or text.** You need to make sure you really thoroughly understand the original text so you can truly summarise the facts and tone of the original piece **without offering interpretation or judgement.**

**Introduction** – Give information about the original essay and a one-sentence summary.

**Body –** Covers the main points of the text. Use paragraphs/chapters as a guide – make at least one point for each.

**No Conclusion** – as it's a summary with no interpretation, there is no need for a conclusion

## CRITIQUE ESSAY STRUCTURE

A critique essay **evaluates a text or other piece of media/ creative work, and reveals the overall meaning through analysis.** You will need to make sure you have a thorough understanding of the subject text/work, and be able to observe details – you should use these (passages or details) as evidence to support your points. **This is not the same as a review, which gives advice.**

**Introduction** – Give information about the subject piece and a one-sentence summary of its general point or purpose. Outline the point you are going to make about it..

**Body** – about 3 paragraphs work chronologically through the piece, picking out points that covering the piece's story arc, greater meaning, or message.

**Conclusion** – summarise your overall argument, perhaps offering a view of why the author/ director (etc.) might have wanted this view to come across.

## DESCRIPTIVE ESSAY STRUCTURE

A descriptive essay is often mistaken for being a short story, which would have a beginning, middle and an end with a plot running through it. Instead, a descriptive essay has a beginning, middle and end but just describes a person, object or place.

**In order to write a good descriptive essay, concrete detail should be used instead of abstract detail** *(like the types of noun in chapter 1)*, **in order to give the reader a more vivid understanding of the topic.**

**A good basic structure uses the five senses.**

**Introduction** – introduce your topic, giving a time and place setting to help start you off.

**First Section** – give concrete details using the sense of **sight**; what does it/do they look like?

**Second Section** – give concrete details using the sense of **hearing**; what sounds are associated with it? If a person, what do they sounds like?

**Third Section** – give concrete details using the sense of **touch** if it's an object or a place – how does it feel? – or their **actions** if it's a person.

**(Fourth and Fifth Sections** – give concrete details using the sense of smell and taste IF RELEVANT to the subject)

**CONCLUSION** – give your overall feelings towards the subject that finalises your description of it.

## PERSUASIVE ESSAY STRUCTURE

Whether you are writing a persuasive speech, a for-or-against essay, or a (dis) proving the statement essay, there is one thing you need: a strong argument.

**In essence, that is what this structure shows you how to create.**

**PERSUASIVE ESSAYS:** these often take on the form of a speech, letter or article, intended to give an opinion on an important topic.

**FOR/AGAINST ESSAYS:** these either give you a point of view to uphold and argue – like a debate – or ask you to take a particular stance on a topic and argue it. **Present the weaker argument first, then the stronger one so the conclusion sounds natural.**

**(DIS)PROVE THE STATEMENT ESSAYS:** similarly to For/Against essays, you will be given a view on the text or topic you are studying and asked how far you agree with it.

**All of these structures involve supporting your view with evidence and proving it to be stronger over any other argument or view.**

**Introduction** – introduce your topic, giving its outline, and give an overview of the view / argument in the essay title

**First Section** – give the first point of one side of the argument/your view, backed up with evidence.

**Second Section** – give the second point of one side of the argument/your view, backed up with evidence.

**Third Section –** give the third point of one side of the argument/your view, backed up with evidence. **By now, this argument should sound strong.**

**Fourth Section** – give the alternative side of the argument/another viewpoint (a counter-argument) *If you are writing a persuasive essay,* next **undermine it to apparently strengthen your own view.**

**CONCLUSION –** summarise the main points of both sides of the argument/both views, and show which you believe is the stronger.

Use these features: A  F O R E S T

A - **A**lliteration
F - **F**acts
O – **O**pinions
R - **R**epetition / **R**hetorical Questions
E - **E**xamples / **E**xperts
S - **S**tatistics
T - lists of **T**hree

## UNIVERSITY PERSONAL STATEMENT STRUCTURE

A Personal Statement is one of the most important documents you'll ever write, and getting the structure right is crucial.

Although you should look at good examples before you write your own, here is a good structure to follow.

**Remember, for UK UCAS University entries, there is a 4000 character (NOT word!) limit, so remember to check this on a word processing program before you input it into the website form!**

**There is no substitute for participating in extra-curricular activities and being well-read in your chosen field – these will both give you something interesting to talk about in your statement that your interviewer may pick up on, giving you a chance to shine out from other candidates.**

**Introduction** – introduce yourself, your subject, and the particular aspects of it you find most interested in.

**Paragraph 1:** What have you done/studied in relation to the subject that's not on your UCAS form?

**Paragraph 2:** your interests (curricular) that link to your subject and which aren't already on your UCAS form.

**Paragraph 3:** your interests (extra-curricular) that link to your subject and which aren't already on your UCAS form.

**Paragraph 4:** work experience, trips or responsibilities (e.g.: school council) that are relevant to the subject.

**PARAGRAPH 5:** your other interests/activities/jobs outside of school that show you to reliable/responsible/ a good citizen

**CONCLUSION** – why you want to attend (that) University and what you hope to gain. Finish with something memorable!

Well done!

Bert is
pleased
with your
progress.

☺

Get more help from Bert at
**blackboardfiction.com/
bertdoesshakespeare**

**This book was brought to you by the fonts**
Century Gothic
Chalkduster
Garamond
Mom's Typewriter by Christophe Mueller
(nonsuch@cuci.nl)
and some typewriter stamps

# How to use **this structure** effectively:

The example you saw on the previous pages is pretty simple. It isn't going to get you much more than a C, perhaps a B if it's combined with a few more excellent pieces of Evidence to support the Point being made. **You'll have to also:**

- **be more sophisticated in your writing**, using a variety of sentence structures and punctuation (especially commas and semicolons) confidently. **So practise!**

- **dig deeper to explain the author's choices** of words and their connotations (*next chapter*).

- **provide more than one piece of evidence** to support each paragraph point.

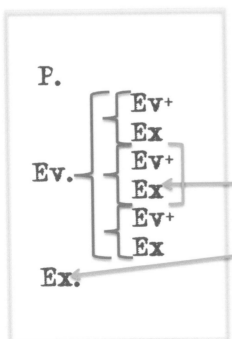

**This paragraph's structure has been developed further.** Instead of simply one piece of Evidence and one Explanation, the Evidence for the Point has several **explained quotations** and an overall Explanation (a bit like a **mini-conclusion**) finishes off this **more sophisticated paragraph**.